Cool
CARS

For Conrad. Cool cars to dream of driving. – T.M.

First published 2005 by Kingfisher
This edition published 2013 by Macmillan Children's Books
an imprint of Pan Macmillan,
a division of Macmillan Publishers Ltd
20 New Wharf Road, London N1 9RR
Associated companies throughout the world

www.panmacmillan.com

ISBN: 978-1-4472-1264-5

Text copyright © Tony Mitton 2005
Illustrations copyright © Ant Parker 2005

Moral rights asserted.

7 9 8 6

A CIP catalogue record for this book is available from the British Library.

Printed in China

Cool CARS

Tony Mitton
and
Ant Parker

MACMILLAN CHILDREN'S BOOKS

Cars are really handy
for getting us around.
They whizz about on busy roads
and make a zoomy sound.

Cars can come in many shapes,
in sizes large or tiny.
Here's a little mini car
and one that's big and shiny.

A car must have a driver,
to make it start and go.
The roads are full of many things
a driver needs to know.

Traffic lights, road markings,
signs along the way –
you have to read them quickly,
and do the things they say.

The steering wheel directs the car
and turns it left or right.
The mirrors help to keep
the other traffic well in sight.

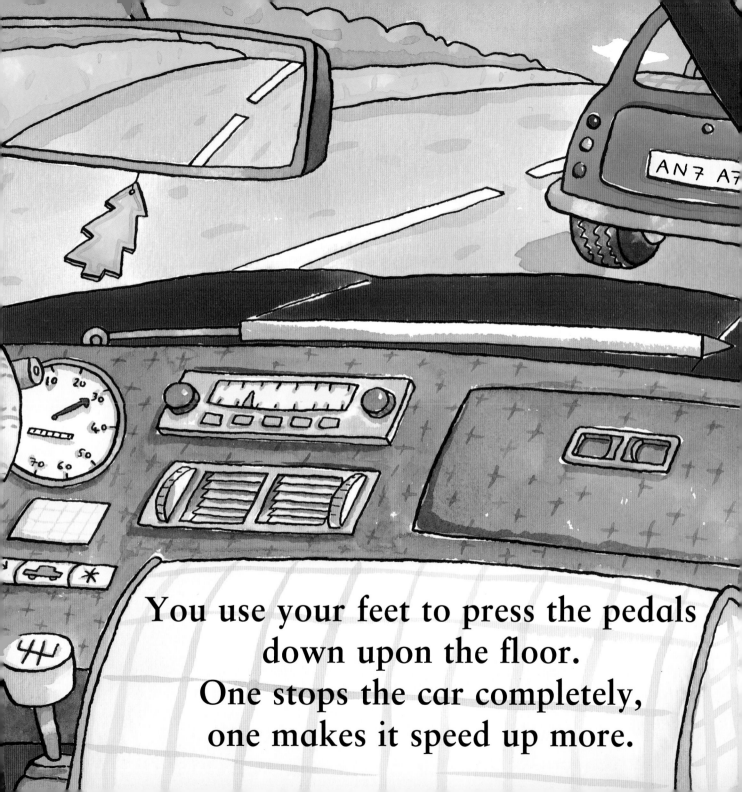

You use your feet to press the pedals
down upon the floor.
One stops the car completely,
one makes it speed up more.

To keep your car in good condition,
give it proper care.
Check the oil, top it up,
and pump the tyres with air.

Fill its tank with fuel,
then drive it through the wash.
The wipers clear the windscreen
with a swishy, swishy, swash!

Convertibles are really great
for driving in the sun.
The top folds down or comes right off.
It makes the drive more fun.

If you're driving off the road,
on ground that's really rough,
a sturdy four-wheel drive is best,
with tyres thick and tough.

Some cars are built for racing.
They zip along so fast.

It's noisy and exciting
as they all go roaring past.

Police cars have a siren
and beacon lights that flash,

to show they're chasing criminals
or helping at a crash.

Some cars are really fancy,
like gleaming limousines.
They're used to carry movie stars
and presidents and queens.

But anyone who's out in town,
and needs to take a ride,
can hail a passing taxicab
and quickly jump inside.

Cars are really popular
for getting us about,

so sometimes there's a traffic jam,
and cars just can't get out.

But when the roads are clear
and the weather's fine and bright,
a journey in the country
can fill us with delight.

We've packed a yummy picnic.
It's a lovely sunny day.
Let's buckle up our safety belts
and then we're on our way.

Car bits

windscreen
the front window gives
the driver a view of
the road ahead

**steering
wheel**
you turn this with
your hands to
direct the car

boot
this is the space for
storing baggage

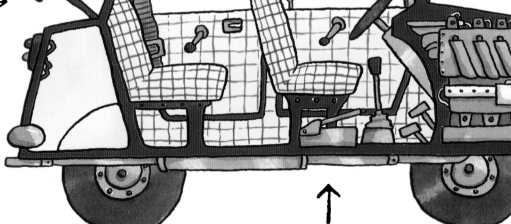

engine
this gives the
power that moves
the car

wheel
this rolls round to
move the car along

handbrake
this is an extra
safety brake to
keep the car still